AF751604

## About Monkey Baa

Monkey Baa Theatre Company was formed in 1997 by Eva Di Cesare, Sandra Eldridge and Tim McGarry. Since then, the company have adapted and staged over fourteen works, three of which have been published. They are renowned for creating quality theatre experiences for young people and being one of Australia's largest touring theatre companies. The company resides at Lend Lease Darling Quarter Theatre, Sydney, NSW. Read more about the company at www.monkeybaa.com.au.

*Jeff Teale (above) as Shaun and Nat Jobe as Pete, in the 2015 Monkey Baa Theatre Company production at the Lend Lease Darling Quarter Theatre, Sydney.* (Photo: Heidrun Löhr)

# Pete the Sheep

## the play

based on the picture book by

Jackie French and Bruce Whatley

adapted for the stage by

Eva Di Cesare, Tim McGarry & Sandra Eldridge

music and lyrics by

Phillip Scott

CURRENCY PRESS
SYDNEY

CURRENCY TEENAGE SERIES

First published in 2015
by Currency Press Pty Ltd,
PO Box 2287, Strawberry Hills, NSW, 2012, Australia.
enquiries@currency.com.au
www.currency.com.au

Copyright: *Pete the Sheep* © Monkey Baa, 2015; lyrics © Phillip Scott, 2015

The Australian Copyright Act 1968 (Act) allows a maximum of one chapter or 10% of this book, whichever is the greater, to be copied by any educational institution for its educational purposes provided that that educational institution (or the body that administers it) has given a remuneration notice to Copyright Agency Limited (CAL) under the Act.

For details of the CAL licence for educational institutions contact
CAL, Level 15/233 Castlereagh Street, Sydney, NSW, 2000;
tel: within Australia 1800 066 844 toll free; outside Australia +61 2 9394 7600;
fax: +61 2 9394 7601; email: info@copyright.com.au

COPYING FOR OTHER PURPOSES

Except as permitted under the Act, for example a fair dealing for the purposes of study, research, criticism or review, no part of this book may be reproduced, stored in a retrieval system, or transmitted in any form or by any means without prior written permission. All enquiries should be made to the publisher at the address above.

Any performance or public reading of *Pete the Sheep* is forbidden unless a licence has been received from the author and the composer The purchase of this book in no way gives the purchaser the right to perform the play in public, whether by means of a staged production or a reading. All applications for public performance should be addressed to Monkey Baa Theatre Company, Lend Lease Darling Quarter Theatre Terrace 3, 1-25 Harbour Street, Sydney NSW 2000; tel. +61 2 8624 9341; fax: +61 2 8209 7977 email: admin@monkeybaa.com.au

Please note that any performance of *Pete the Sheep* must include the original compositions by Phillip Scott. For the original score, please get in touch with HMMG Pty Ltd, Fox Studios Australia, FSA #38, 38 Driver Avenue, Moore Park NSW 2021; tel. +61 2 8353 2444; email hmm@harrymmiller.com.

Cataloguing-in-publication data for this title is available from the National Library of Australia website: www.nla.gov.au

Typeset for Currency Press by Dean Nottle.
Printed by Ligare Book Printers, Riverwood NSW.
Cover designed by Emma Vine for Currency Press.

## Foreword: A black sheep's journey

Once upon a time there was a sheep called… Dunmore. A black sheep, who would round up the other sheep in return for a milk arrowroot biscuit. But the drought was bad, and grass had vanished. So we came up with a scheme. We'd give a sheep to every school in Australia, where they could eat the grassy ovals, and we'd become a team of shearers giving them stunning haircuts.

Luckily the drought broke before we tried it.

But the memory became a picture book, with Dunmore transformed into Pete the Sheep with the genius of Bruce Whatley. And the brilliance of Monkey Baa Theatre Company, and Sandie, Eva and Tim, with composer Phil Scott turned the book into a musical, directed by Jonathan Biggins, that danced across Australia.

But somehow, deeply, wonderfully, the play captured the mateship and desperation and dreams from the place the book began. Monkey Baa is always – always – magic.

*Jackie French*

*From left: Todd Keys as Sheep One, Jeff Teale (obscured) as Sheep Three, Nat Jobe as Pete and Andrew James as Sheep Two in the 2015 Monkey Baa Theatre Company production at the Lend Lease Darling Quarter Theatre, Sydney.* (Photo: Heidrun Löhr)

## Contents

*To Jonathan and Phil for being such hilarious and inspiring collaborators.*

## A note from the adaptors

*Pete the Sheep* is a tale that challenges stereotypes, celebrates difference and reflects 'mateship' in contemporary Australia. In developing the picture book for the stage we wanted to create and reflect a world that still is very much part of rural Australia. Shearers are not just historical figures that live in folklore or are represented in framed oil paintings. They are a part of our contemporary landscape, although their world still has echoes of yesteryear. We wanted audiences, and in particular our regional and remote audiences, to experience this world in a contemporary theatre piece. The world of the shearing shed is not some piece of mythology dragged back from the pages of history. It is a valid albeit conservative world, and therefore a great place to challenge themes of difference and generational change. After all – you can now do a certificate course at TAFE in shearing!

We were drawn to this particular story because at its heart lies the continuing battle for tolerance and integrity and the resounding lesson for us all that diversity can make our lives richer and… give us fabulous haircuts!

We had never worked with young people in the script development process of our plays in such depth, and wanted to engage more deeply with them in the early stage of the script development. In working with Year Five students from Our Lady of Mount Carmel and Fort Street Public School on themes and characters from the book, their perspective and interpretation very much guided our interpretation and development of theme. Spending a week in the Araluen Valley meeting with shearers, learning the lingo and and the workings of a shed gave us enormous material both in language and also design. Music was also an element that resonated loudly in our imaginations, and the prowess and talent of Phil Scott, his lyrics and music propelled the story to new heights.

To bring it all together, we couldn't go past Jonathan Biggins. His vision and guidance throughout the entire process was inspiring.

And of course, spending time with Jackie French, 'chewing the fat' and delving deeper into character and story became the richest source of all.

She is our hero.

*Eva Di Cesare, Sandra Eldridge and Tim McGarry*

## First production

*Pete the Sheep* was first produced by Monkey Baa Theatre Company at their home, the Lend Lease Darling Quarter Theatre, Sydney, on 29 March 2014 with the following cast:

| | |
|---|---|
| **RATSO, TINY, SHEEP** | Andrew James |
| **BUNGO, PETE** | Nat Jobe |
| **BIG BOB, BRUTE, SHEEP** | Todd Keys |
| **SHAUN, FANG, SHEEP** | Jeff Teale |

Director, Jonathan Biggins
Composer & Lyricist, Phillip Scott
Set & Costume Designer, James Browne
Lighting Designer, Matthew Marshall
Sound Designer, Kingsley Reeve

*Pete the Sheep* toured to 54 theatre venues throughout Australia in 2014.

*From left: Jeff Teale as Shaun, Andrew James as Ratso, Todd Keys as Brute and Nat Jobe as Bungo in the 2015 Monkey Baa Theatre Company production at the Lend Lease Darling Quarter Theatre, Sydney.*
*(Photo: Heidrun Löhr)*

## Director's note

*Pete the Sheep* is an uncomplicated story set in an uncomplicated world and any theatrical adaptation needs to honour the book's cleverly naïve simplicity. So when we began to bring to the stage the story of a sheep with a fondness for coiffure, we kept it deliberately simple in setting and style – corrugated iron, blue singlets, old timber floors and four actors playing all the shearers, sheep and dogs.

Some things we had to change – picture books and plays have different narrative arcs and once we'd reached the hair salon, we couldn't really go back as they do in the book. But a few structural tweaks here and there and the invention of Shaun's 'midnight shear' solved those problems. And, of course, the music and lyrics of Phil Scott gave us a fantastic new element for storytelling and engagement.

But most importantly, we gave the kids a glimpse of a world they're perhaps not familiar with; one without screens, technology and distraction. And by putting in a few jokes for the adults in the audience, we had a show that the whole family could enjoy – nothing engages a young audience as much as knowing the grown-ups are having a good time as well.

And the theme of the book is ageless: tolerance and inclusion always bring out the best in us all. There's more than one way to shear a sheep and everyone, four-legged or not, likes to feel a bit special. It was a pleasure to help transform this wonderful book into an equally wonderful show – long may the Shaggy Gully Dream Team knock about the country's sheds and stages!

*Jonathan Biggins*

## Acknowledgements

The adaptors wish to thank Jackie French and Bruce Whatley for their beautiful story that touches so many hearts, making us laugh and cry.

Thank you to Jackie for her continued support, encouragement and trust in Monkey Baa and to her and Bryan for letting us stay in the magical valley during our research.

We would also like to thank Pete and Jamie Raynolds for their hospitality, tour of their farm and all the tips on shearing and shed culture.

To the students of Year 5/6 from Our Lady of Mount Carmel, Waterloo and Fort Street Public School, Millers Point, we thank you from the bottom of our hearts for your incredible insight.

## Characters

**SHAUN:** A young, new shearer from out of town. Shaun is from a poor background and as a boy was given a sheep instead of a dog. Shaun has recently completed a TAFE degree in shearing. He is very polite, very creative and has a special bond with his sheep, Pete. They are the best of friends. Shaun just does things differently.

**PETE:** A polite sheep and Shaun's best mate. The world is not a puzzle to Pete; he is an individual who treats everyone, including fellow sheep, with respect. Pete's a leader not a follower who has many bright ideas which he articulately shares. He wears Shaun's hat.

**RATSO:** The ringer, gunner and the best shearer in town. All that's important to him is the world according to Ratso. 'There's only one way. My way.' Ratso yells a lot and runs his shed with a no-nonsense, black and white view of the world. Ratso has a sheepdog called Brute.

**BIG BOB**: He loves dogs! Wherever his dog Tiny goes, he does. A passionate defender of sheepdogs and their role in the shearing shed. Big Bob gets genuinely distressed that a dog can be replaced by a sheep. He is more open to change than Ratso and gets quite excited. He has a very loud voice and tends to yell.

**BUNGO:** He is the strong silent type and doesn't have much to say. When he does speak, he is a mutterer. He is really a follower not a leader. Bungo has a dog called Fang.

**BRUTE:** Ratso's dog… Woof! He's Ratso's best mate. An

obedient working dog who is at his master's side all day when not rounding up the sheep. Suffers occasionally from worms and often scratches at his fleas and licks parts of his body. In Shaun's Sheep Salon, Brute favours a soft curl perm.

**TINY:** Big Bob's dog… Arf arff arfff! The smallest dog of the pack who plays a mean blues harmonica as his alter ego Blind Tiny Footsteps. A sufferer of fleas, he is often found scratching. In Shaun's Sheep Salon, Tiny favours a 60's set bouffant.

**FANG:** Bungo's dog… Grrrrrrr! He eats flies out of the air, snaps at them constantly, when he's not scratching at his fleas. In Shaun's Sheep Salon, Fang favours a 70's punk new wave.

**SHEEP:** True merino. They walk in single file. They look down when distressed. Bleating or baaaing is used as a way of making contact, communicating. They see in colour and have a panoramic view.

## Setting

The play is set inside and outside the shearing shed on a sheep farm in Shaggy Gully, rural Australia.

And… inside and outside Shaun's Sheep Salon, a hairdressing salon in the Shaggy Gully township.

# Prologue

*Theatre foyer.*

*Venues will be encouraged to set their foyers up in the style of the play.*

*Celebration of the shearing way of life – hay bales, eucalyptus trees, fencing, memorabilia from shearing sheds, etc.*

*It is hoped local schools will display artwork commemorating the world of Pete the Sheep.*

*Country music feel to the front of house music.*

*Two shearers,* **RATSO** *and* **BUNGO**, *appear with their dogs,* **BRUTE** *and* **FANG**. **RATSO** *whistles.*

**RATSO**: Brute!
**BUNGO**: Fang!
**RATSO & BUNGO**: Round 'em up!
**BRUTE**: Woof. Woof!
**FANG**: Grrrr.

> **BRUTE** *tries to cock his leg and relieve himself on one of the audience members.*

**RATSO**: Git away from there. Whaddayathink this is? Bush week?
**BUNGO**: Check out the fleece on this one.
**RATSO**: Bunch of rejects from the Tamworth [*insert local town reference here*] Show here for sure.

> **BUNGO** *refers to another audience member.*

**BUNGO**: This'll get a good price. Plenty o' yarn.
**RATSO**: Ooh, yeah. Enough to knit a scarf from here to the back o' Bourke!

*They exit as the audience moves into the auditorium and are seated.*

*As the audience enter the auditorium a pre-show bush farm soundscape is heard – sheep, cockatoos, beautiful bird sounds, magpies.*

*As the lights go down…*

*Voices come over the PA system (in a sheep accent), accompanied by the sound of a tapping hoof and blowing 'fff-fff' through the microphone:*

**AUNT WOOLLY**: Is this on?

**SHAUN**: Yes, Aunt Woolly.

**AUNT WOOLLY**: G'daaaay, ewes and wethers, welcome to Shaggy Gully. No chewing or eating in the shearing shed. And no photos – our sheep are very shyyyy… and don't be a dag – turn off your mobile phones. Now… sit back, relax, and enjoy the show brought to ewes by Monkey Baaaa.

**SHAUN**: Thanks, Aunt Woolly.

## Scene One

*Shearing shed interior. Monday morning.*

*Sunrise.*

*Morning sounds – rooster, cockatoos, a cacophony of bird noises and the bleating of sheep.*

**RATSO** *enters. He rings the bell.*

***SONG ONE: 'Three Shearers'***

**RATSO**: *G'day there, everybody.*
*You're gonna hear a little yarn.*

*All about how to shear a sheep*
*And the proper way it's done.*

*So my name's Ratso, I'm the boss,*
*The bloke they call the gunner.*
*We shear the sheep from dawn till dusk*
*On both sides and down unner.*

**SHEARERS**: *We work real hard all day (all day)*
*And this is what we say: we say...*

*Mate! Mate! Hey, mate! Mate! Mate! Hey, mate!*
*The clippers are goin' at a one two three.*
*Keep 'em comin' till we break for a cup of tea.*

**BIG BOB**: *Gaa-day there, everybody.*
*The fellers call me Big Bob.*
*I'm the second best shearer in this town:*
*That's the second most important job!*
*And this here's Bungo, he's my mate,*

**BUNGO**: [*spoken*] Yep.

**BIG BOB**: *He ain't got a lot to say.*

**BUNGO**: [*spoken*] Nup.

**BIG BOB**: *But you can trust him with your life –*
*If not with two weeks' pay.*

**BUNGO**: [*spoken*] Hang on.

**RATSO**: *Keep workin', don't relax (relax)*
*Till the wool is off their backs. We say:*

**VARIOUS**: *Mate! Mate! Hey, mate! Mate! Mate! Hey, mate!*
*The clippers are goin' at a one two three.*
*Keep 'em comin' till we break for a cup of tea.*

*The shearers morph into dogs (***SHAUN** *is* **FANG**, **BIG BOB** *is* **BRUTE**, **RATSO** *is* **TINY**.*)*

**FANG**: *G'day there, everybody.*
*We're sheepdogs through and through.*
*I'm Fang!*
**BRUTE**: *I'm Brute!*
**TINY**: *I'm Tiny…*
**FANG**: *With a special job to do.*
*We keep the flock together,*
*Go after every stray.*
*And if any silly sheep makes a dash for the gate*
*We are there to block its way.*
**ALL**: *A sheep is not real smart (real smart)*
**FANG**: *But rounding 'em up's an art.*
**ALL**: *We go:*
*Ruff! Ruff! Ruff, ruff! Ruff! Ruff! Ruff, ruff!*
*Keep them moving in a single line,*
*Sheepdogs rule! We're a part of the grand design.*

*The dogs morph into three sheep.*

**SHEEP THREE & FOUR**: [*in unison*] *G'day there, everybody.*
*We're sheep who have no name.*
*We love to stand and stare at the ground.*

*Long pause while they do.*

**SHEEP ONE**: *And we all act just the same.*
**SHEEP THREE & FOUR**: *And we all act just the same.*
**ALL**: *Our wool is highly prized, of course,*
*Cos we are prime merinos.*
*The wool goes overseas, but where*
*Is something only he knows.*

*Where? Where? Where? We're…*
*… scared of every beast,*

*That's why we're easily fleeced.*
*Crying: Baa-baa. Baa-baa. Baa Baa. Baa-baa.*

**SHEEP ONE**: *Our favourite pastime's doing poos.*
*Our brains are small, so we are a lot like ewes.*

*One sheep stays* [**SHAUN**]. *The other two morph back* **into RATSO** *and* **BRUTE**.

**BUNGO** *re-enters.*

**RATSO**: *A shearer's life's a hard one*
*In this tough Australian scene,*
*With the boss*
**BUNGO**: *And the boys*
**BRUTE**: *And the dogs*
**SHEEP**: [**SHAUN**] *And the sheep*
**ALL**: *It's how it's always been.*
**RATSO**: *We make it run like clockwork*
*Right through the shearing season,*
**ALL**: *We know things are never gonna change.*
**BUNGO**: *Can't see any blinking reason!*
**ALL**: *Each player knows his place.*
**OTHERS**: *His place.*
**RATSO & BUNGO**: *It's always been the case.*
**ALL**: *We go:*
**RATSO**: *Mate!*
**BRUTE**: *Ruff!*
**BUNGO**: *Yeah?*
**BRUTE**: *Ruff!*
**SHEEP**: *Baa.*
**BRUTE**: *Ruff, ruff!*
**RATSO**: *Mate!*

**SHEEP**: *Baa.*

**RATSO**: *Mate!*

**BRUTE**: *Ruff!*

**BUNGO**: *Yeah?*

**RATSO**: *Mate!*

**SHEEP**: *Baa.*

**BRUTE**: *Ruff!*

**ALL**: *Clippers are goin' at a one two three.*
*Keep 'em comin' till we break for a nice sweet pot of billy tea.*

**BRUTE**: [*aside*] *And a great big bone for me.*

**RATSO** *rings the bell and calls out the roster.*

**RATSO**: Okay, fellas. Time to call the roster. Big Bob?

**BIG BOB**: Present and accounted for.

**RATSO**: Ratso? Ratso? Hang on a minute, that's me. Present.

**RATSO**: Bungo?

**BUNGO**: Too right.

**RATSO**: Shaun?

*No response.*

**RATSO**: Shaun?

**BIG BOB**: Who?

**RATSO**: [*checking the roster*] Some joker called Shaun. Looks like Boss Cocky's put on a new bloke.

**BIG BOB**: Well, where is he?

**RATSO**: Dunno. Must have lost his watch.

**BIG BOB**: How did you work that out?

**RATSO**: Cos he's late, ya drongo.

**BUNGO**: Strewth.

**BIG BOB**: Jumping jumbucks. We're gonna be one shearer down if this bloke doesn't front up.

**RATSO**: And there's three thousand sheep in the back paddock... [*pointing to the audience*] and there's over a thousand in that paddock.

**BIG BOB**: If this Shaun's a no-show, that's over three hundred sheep we gotta shear a day.

**RATSO**: Each.

**BUNGO**: Strewth.

**BIG BOB**: That's more than we've ever done in a day, Ratso. Even on me best days, I'm pushing to get out two fifty.

**RATSO**: Well, we can't wait any longer. We're starting without him. Right crank it up, boys.

*Machinery starts up.*

*The shearers get ready to shear.*

**SHAUN** *arrives.*

*He tries to get their attention by waving.* **BUNGO** *notices him, taps* **RATSO** *on the shoulder.*

*A mime sequence occurs.*

**SHAUN**: Morning. Good morning. Good MOR...NING!

*The shearers all stop.*

*The machinery stops just as* **SHAUN** *is yelling out his last 'morning'.*

**SHAUN**: Morning. Sorry. The bus was late. A truck lost its load just out of town and traffic was banked right up to...

**RATSO**: Let me guess. Shaun?

**SHAUN**: Too right. Pleased to meet you.

**RATSO**: Yeah. G'day. I'm Ratso, I'm the ringer. This here is Big Bob and that's Bungo.

**SHAUN**: Pleased to meet you all. Do you have a fridge?

*He indicates his lunch box.*

**SHAUN**: Microwave?

*He indicates his mobile phone.*

**SHAUN**: Wi-fi?

**BUNGO**: Strewth.

**RATSO**: I run a tight shed here. Bus or no bus, you're late! We start at seven-thirty sharp. We break at ten for elevenses, twelve for lunch, three for tea and five you're free. Your grub's supplied so leave your tin at home. There's a tap if you're dry. And you can turn that mobile off. No wi-fi within cooee of here, mate.

**BUNGO**: Cooeee!

*From left: Jeff Teale as Shaun, Nat Jobe as Bungo and Andrew James as Ratso in the 2015 Monkey Baa Theatre Company production at the Lend Lease Darling Quarter Theatre, Sydney.* (Photo: Heidrun Löhr)

**BIG BOB**: No-one to hear you scream.

**SHAUN**: Great.

**RATSO**: You're gonna be working with as good a bunch of shearers as you'll ever work with.

**SHAUN**: I'm really looking forward to starting.

**RATSO**: Later on today we're doing the rams and they're worth a few quid. There's a ram in that paddock that's won prize ribbons at the Royal Easter Show. [*Or change to a local town show.*] So be careful with their... bits.

**BIG BOB**: Y'up for it?

**SHAUN**: I've done a certificate course at TAFE.

**BIG BOB**: Where?

**SHAUN**: The college of Technical and Further Education back home. I topped the class.

**BUNGO** *exits.*

**BIG BOB**: Dead set?

**SHAUN**: I was in the Gifted and Talented.

**BIG BOB**: Yeah. But are you any good?

**SHAUN**: I seem to have a gift. My dad and my granddad were both shearers. It's in my blood.

**BIG BOB**: Really? I've been doing a correspondence course meself, ya know... on ancestry... quite interesting...

**RATSO**: Righto. Righto. Enough gas bagging. Let's get to work. Where's your sheepdog?

**SHAUN**: Oh, he was just behind me. [*He whistles.*] Pete!

**PETE** *enters. He's a sheep.*

**PETE**: Baaaaaaa.

**SHAUN**: I know, Pete. I'm really excited too. [*To* **RATSO**] This is Pete.

**RATSO**: I said where's your sheepdog.

**SHAUN**: [*pointing at* **PETE**] Here.

**RATSO**: That's not a dog. That's a sheep.

**SHAUN**: Yeah. He's a sheep-sheep.

**RATSO**: A what?

**SHAUN**: A sheep-sheep.

**PETE**: Baaaa. Baaaa.

**SHAUN**: That's alright, Pete. I've explained about the bus.

**RATSO**: You're pullin' my leg.

**SHAUN**: Sorry?

**RATSO**: That's not a sheepdog.

**SHAUN**: He's *like* a sheepdog.

**RATSO**: He's nothing like a sheepdog! Brute!

**BRUTE** *appears.*

**BRUTE**: Woof. Woof. Woof. Woof.

**RATSO**: Sit... beg... shake hands.

**BRUTE** *does as instructed.*

**RATSO**: Now, that's a sheepdog!

**SHAUN** *and* **PETE** *look at each other.*

**SHAUN**: We can do that. Pete?

**PETE**: Baaaa. [*As in: Are you serious?*]

**SHAUN**: If you don't mind, little buddy.

**PETE**: Baaa. [*Pleading: Really?*]

**SHAUN**: I know I know. But when in Roma... sit... beg... shake.

**PETE** *does all of these but in his own special way and nothing like* **BRUTE**.

**SHAUN**: That'll do, sheep, that'll do. [*To* **RATSO**] And that's a sheep-sheep!

**RATSO**: Are you havin' a lend of me?

**SHAUN**: Oh no. I'm perfectly serious. He's a sheep-sheep. My mum couldn't afford a dog but she gave me Pete. He's an orphan. We've been together for years.

**RATSO**: You can't have a sheep-sheep.

**SHAUN**: Pete's as good as any sheepdog, believe me.

**RATSO**: Fair dinkum? Brute! [*He whistles.*] Get out into that back paddock and cut me out a sheep.

**BRUTE** *goes off.*

**SHAUN**: A sheep-sheep just does things differently. Same result though.

**PETE**: Baaaaa.

**RATSO**: Look, mate, I don't care if he's a sheep-sheep, sheep-pig, sheep-chicken – up first in the morning. He doesn't belong here! My shed! My rules!

**BRUTE** *woofs offstage and* **SHEEP ONE** *appears.*

**RATSO** *rough handles* **SHEEP ONE** *who struggles.*

**RATSO**: Come here, you ewe.

**RATSO** *demonstrates the shearing to show how it's really done.*

**RATSO**: That's how it is. And that's how I want it done.

**RATSO** *pushes the* **SHEEP** *back out into the paddock.* **SHEEP ONE** *exits.*

**SHAUN**: Good-oh. We can do that.

**RATSO**: So Mr Gifted and Talented. Show us what you've got.

**SHAUN**: Certainly. Pete. Would you kindly fetch me a sheep?

**RATSO**: Give me strength!

**PETE** *exits to get a sheep.* **PETE** *and* **SHEEP TWO** *reappear.*

**PETE** *speaks politely to the* **SHEEP**.

**PETE**: Baaa. Step this way please, madam.
**SHEEP TWO**: Baaa... what?
**PETE**: How was your day today?
**SHEEP TWO**: Er... well... same as every other day, I guess.
**PETE**: Now... how about we take a little bit off the top?
**SHEEP TWO**: Ooh. That'd be lovely. You're so much nicer than those barking dogs.

*The* **SHEEP** *gently walks up to* **SHAUN** *to be shorn.*

**SHAUN** *and* **PETE** *show their unique shearing style.*

***SONG TWO: 'Shaun's First Shear'***

**SHAUN**: *Show you how it's done.*
*With a bit of style.*
*This is what I learnt at Tech.*
**PETE**: [*to a* **SHEEP** *being shorn*] *Yes, he learnt it at Tech.*
**SHAUN**: *Clipper number one.*
*Don't forget to smile.*
*Careful not to nick the neck.*

*He does. The* **SHEEP** *reacts.*

**PETE**: *Oops. How's the neck?*
**SHAUN**: *Snip, snip, clip, clip, clip.*
*She'll be smooth as newborn kittens,*
*Lots of wool for scarves and mittens.*
*When you get a sheep,*
*Hold her like a friend,*
*And you'll find the hours will fly.*
**PETE**: [*to the* **SHEEP**] *How the hours will fly.*
**SHAUN**: *You won't hear a peep*
*Out of either end.*

*Makes it hard to say goodbye!*

**PETE**: *There's a tear in his eye.*

**SHAUN**: [*finishing up*] *Clip, clip, snip, snip, snip, snip.*
*Sheep and shearer work together,*
*There's the wool and there's your wether.*
*Why*
*Not give it a try?*
*Ay yi yi!*

**RATSO**: Well… I've seen some weird things in my day, but that takes the biscuit.

**SHEEP TWO**: Baaaa.

*From left: Nat Jobe as Pete, Jeff Teale as Shaun and Todd Keys as Sheep in the 2015 Monkey Baa Theatre Company production at the Lend Lease Darling Quarter Theatre, Sydney.* (Photo: Heidrun Löhr)

**SHAUN**: My pleasure. See, that's how it's done.

**SHEEP TWO**: Baaa. Oh, I've never had a shear like that before.

**PETE**: Baaa. Next time I'll get him to take a little more off around the ears.

**SHEEP TWO**: Such a gentleman. I've never been treated so gently with such care. Thank you. All the other shearers treat us like animals. Well, not anymore! I'm telling the rest of the flock. We're not going to set foot in this shed until we're treated with respect. Girls! Girls! Girls!

**SHEEP TWO** *exits baaaaing excitedly.* **PETE** *follows her.*

*Excited sheep can be heard gossiping in the back paddock.*

**RATSO**: What's going on with those sheep? Brute, sort 'em out.

*He calls out to* **BRUTE** *who is offstage.*

**BRUTE**: [*from off*] Woof woof woof.

*From his barking we can tell that* **BRUTE** *is struggling with the sheep.*

**BUNGO** *enters and joins* **RATSO**.

**BIG BOB** *enters, scratching his head.*

**BIG BOB**: What's up with the sheep? Brute can't shift them.

**RATSO**: What? I'm smelling trouble, boys. And when I smell trouble... there's trouble.

**BUNGO**: Strewth.

**BIG BOB**: Reckon we oughta have a meeting?

**RATSO**: Meeting! Meeting. Any apologies?

**BIG BOB**: Sorry?

**RATSO**: Accepted. Item one. Why aren't those mongrel sheep moving?

**BIG BOB**: I dunno, Ratso. Look at the rest of them.

*They refer to the audience.*

**BUNGO**: Like a flock of stunned mullets.

**RATSO**: That one there looks like a roo caught in the headlights of a ute.

**BIG BOB**: That one looks like a galah hitting a window.

**BUNGO**: Could be the newcomer.

**RATSO**: I think you're onto something, Bungo.

**BUNGO**: Strewth.

**RATSO**: Come on, boys. I'm gonna sort this out once and for all. All those in favour?

**BIG BOB & BUNGO**: A...

**RATSO**: The 'ayes' have it. [*To* **SHAUN**] Right. Me and the boys, we've had a vote.

**BIG BOB**: A vote?

**SHAUN**: Have we done something wrong?

**RATSO**: The question is, mate, have you done anything right?

**SHAUN**: Pete and I, well... we just do things differently.

**RATSO**: We've decided that it's a little too different for us. This shed's always run like clockwork. We've been shearing sheep since 1788 in this country and we shearers have always followed tradition. Shearers have dogs. Dogs round up the sheep. The sheep get shorn. This sheep-sheep of yours is nothing but trouble.

**BIG BOB**: Nothing but trouble.

**RATSO**: He's gotta go.

**BUNGO**: Gotta go.

**SHAUN**: That hardly seems very fair. You haven't given him a chance. This is his first day.

**RATSO**: And here's a newsflash for you, mate... it's his last!

**SHAUN**: But there are lots of ways to shear a sheep.

**RATSO**: See, that's where you're wrong. There's only one way to shear a sheep. And it's our way! Tradition, mate. Tradition.

**BIG BOB**: Tradition. A good dog rounds up the sheep, it doesn't stand around gasbagging to them.

**SHAUN**: Pete can't go.

**RATSO**: Take a good hard look at yourself, son. And get yourself a proper sheepdog!

**SHAUN**: But he's my mate, my rock. He's my right-hand lamb.

**RATSO**: That sheep-sheep is wrong. You're wrong. It's all wrong!

**SHAUN**: Well, if Pete goes, I go!

**RATSO**: Suit yourself. You, ya lunch box, ya wi-fi and your sheep-sheep can rack off outta this shed.

**RATSO, BUNGO** *and* **BIG BOB** *exit.*

**SHAUN** *and* **PETE** *exit the shed.*

## Scene Two

*Outside the shearing shed.*

***SONG THREE: 'Shaun's Lament'***

*A sad little tune in 3/4 time.*

**SHAUN**: *Dear, oh dear.*
*Turfed out of here.*
*But what am I s'posed to do?*
*I've been to school,*

**PETE** *enters.*

*But they think I'm a fool.*
*Yet it couldn't be clearer,*
*I've got to be a shearer,*

*And I'll make a great shearer too!*
*Poor old Shaun*
*Came the raw prawn,*
*And I'll have to cop it sweet.*

**PETE**: [*confused by the idiom*] *Baaaaa?*

**SHAUN**: *Studied for years,*
*Got some great new ideas –*
*But I never expected*
*My ideas'd get rejected*
*Because of my little mate Pete!*

**PETE**: *Baa, baa baa baaa?*

**SHAUN**: *Sorry, mate. We know our fate.*
*We ought to be hitting the trail.*
*If I can't shear*
*We had best disappear.*
*And I don't care what some say –*
*But what'll poor old Mum say*
*When I tell her her son,*
*Her one and only one,*
*Has just got a big F for Fail?*
*Come on, young Pete. Let's bail.*

**SHAUN** *gives a big sigh at the end of the song.* **PETE** *looks at him.*

**PETE**: Baaa.

**PETE** *returns with* **SHAUN***'s lunchbox and offers him some food and brings his clippers.*

**SHAUN**: Thanks, Pete, my little buddy, but I am too depressed to eat.

**PETE**: Baaaaaa baaaaa?

**SHAUN**: Yeah, I don't mind, help yourself.

**PETE**: Baaaaa?

**SHAUN**: No, it's not lamb, it's vegetarian.

**PETE**: Baaa. Baaa baaa.

**SHAUN**: You're right, Pete. It's not fair. They don't know me. But shearing's the only thing I can do. My dad, my granddad. It's in my blood… Well… at least I have you to shear.

**SHAUN** *shears* **PETE**.

***REPRISE: 'Shaun's Lament'***

**SHAUN**: *Something new,*
*That's what I'll do.*
*What have I got to lose?*
*Longer on top.*
*Give that the chop.*
*Cut it and style it*
*And colour it in violet*

**PETE** : *Ba-ba. [As in: Nuh-uh]*

**SHAUN**: *That is the look I would choose.*
*But I only shear you, not ewes.*

**SHAUN** *packs up all his shearing gear and his lunch, and he exits.*

# Scene Three

*Afternoon.*

*In the farmyard.*

*We see* **PETE** *trotting around, showing off his new do to the audience.* **SHEEP THREE** *and* **SHEEP FOUR** *enter. They are astonished at* **PETE***'s new do.*

**SHEEP FOUR**: What on earth has happened to you?

**PETE**: I've been shorn.

**SHEEP FOUR**: Well, you've had the wool pulled over your eyes, that's for sure.

**SHEEP THREE**: It looks ridiculous!

**SHEEP FOUR**: You can say that again.

**SHEEP THREE**: It looks ridiculous.

**PETE**: What? Why?

*They show him his reflection.*

**PETE**: Whoa! Shaun. You've never done that before. You've nailed it. I love it.

**SHEEP THREE**: It's ludicrous!

*From left: Nat Jobe as Pete, Todd Keys as Sheep One and Andrew James as Sheep Two in the 2015 Monkey Baa Theatre Company production at the Lend Lease Darling Quarter Theatre, Sydney.* (Photo: Heidrun Löhr)

**PETE**: But it's just my fleece, ladies. I'm still me inside. And I think I look pretty cool.

***SONG FOUR: 'Sheep Doo Wop'***

**PETE**: *There's nothing wrong with trying something different.*
*Why should you simply stay the way you are?*
*Nothing wrong with heading in a new direction.*
*You don't get anywhere by saying: Na-a-a-ah.*

*We don't all hear the same music.*

**SHEEP THREE & FOUR**: *Mu-u-usic.*

**PETE**: *We don't all read the same book.*

**SHEEP THREE & FOUR**: *Read?*

**PETE**: *There's nothing wrong with trying something new,*
*Even if it's just a new look.*

*Oh…*
*Do what, do what, do what you wanna do.*
*Try it one way,*
*Try it two.*

**ALL**: *You'll know before long if it's right or wrong,*
*Cos everything you do is up to you.*

**SHEEP THREE**: [*spoken*] No no no no, I just follow the herd.

**SHEEP FOUR**: It's too radical for me.

**SHEEP THREE**: I could never try something that different.

**SHEEP FOUR**: We're sheep, for goodness sake. Not flock stars.

**SHEEP THREE**: We'd look like mutton dressed as lamb.

**PETE**: Come on, ladies. Live a little…

**PETE & SHEEP**: [*sung*] *Baa. Baa. Baa. Baa ba baa, Baa. Baa. Baa. Baa-ba-baa.*

**PETE**: *The usual way is not the only option.*
*Old ways tend to get you just so far.*

*Even sheep and shearers like a few surprises.*
*Reckon it's time to raise the ba-a-a-ar.*
*We don't all eat the same clover.*

**SHEEP THREE & FOUR**: *Don't we?*

**PETE**: *We don't all munch the same grass.*

**SHEEP THREE & FOUR**: *Yes we do.*

**PETE**: *Stop acting sheepish like a bunch of sheep!*
*It's time to get off your...*

**SHEEP THREE & FOUR**: *Baaa! Baaaaaa!!*

**ALL**: [*in close three-part harmony*]
*Do what, do what, do what you wanna do.*
*Try it one way,*
*Try it two.*
*You'll know before long if it's right or wrong,*
*Cos everything you do is up to you.*
*Everything you do is up to.*

**ALL**: Ba-baa, ba ba-ba-baaa.

**PETE**: Everybody, let's try...

**ALL**: ... something new!

**SHEEP FOUR**: Ooh. I bags next shear at the Shaggy Gully shearing shed.

**PETE**: Oh, this isn't a Shaggy Gully shearing shed shear. Shaun's the only shearer who can shave like this.

**SHEEP THREE**: When we get into the Shaggy Gully shearing shed, will it be Shaun's shearing shift?

**PETE**: Shaun doesn't shear at the Shaggy Gully shearing shed anymore.

**SHEEP FOUR**: Surely not.

**PETE**: Shaun's been shafted.

**SHEEP FOUR**: Shifted?

**PETE**: Shut out!
**SHEEP THREE**: Oh, shut up!
**SHEEP FOUR**: Shame on those shearers.
**PETE**: Poor Shaun.
**SHEEP THREE**: Poor us. We'll never get a new do.
**SHEEP FOUR**: And with one shearer down, Shaggy Gully shearing shed's gonna be banked up hour after hour.
**SHEEP THREE**: Day after day.
**SHEEP FOUR**: What a woolly mess!
**PETE**: Sorry ladies… unless…
**SHEEP THREE & FOUR**: Unless?

**PETE**'*s light bulb moment.*

**PETE**: Thank you, ladies. I think you've given me an idea!

## Scene Four

*Shearing shed, interior.*

*Midnight.*

*Midnight music underscore.*

*It's dark and we can only hear voices.*

**PETE**: Baaaa.
**SHAUN**: What is it, Pete? I can't see a thing. I've lost you.
**PETE**: Baaaa.
**SHAUN**: You're going too fast. Wait up. Why have I got this blindfold on? It's not my birthday.
**PETE**: Baaaaa.
**SHAUN**: You've gotta tell me what's going on, Pete.
**PETE**: Baaaaa. Baaaa.

**SHAUN**: Why are we whispering? It's the middle of the night. Hang on, Pete. Where are we going?

**PETE**: Baaaa.

*Moonlight reveals* **PETE** *dragging a blindfolded* **SHAUN** *into the shed.*

**PETE** *removes the blindfold.*

**PETE** *has set up a makeshift hair salon out of a couple of wooden apple boxes.*

*Beside the boxes, there is a mirror and* **SHAUN***'s shearing equipment.*

**SHEEP THREE** *is waiting patiently with dark glasses on (incognito) to have her hair done.*

**SHEEP THREE**: Baaaaa.

**SHAUN**: Pete, what's all this about?

**PETE**: [*to* **SHEEP THREE**] We'll be with you shortly. [*To* **SHAUN**] Baaaa.

**SHAUN**: Moonlighting? Does anyone know we're here?

**PETE**: Baaaa.

**SHAUN**: What if we get caught?

**PETE**: Meh. [*As in: Who cares?*]

**SHAUN**: Whose idea was this?

**PETE**: Ba-baaaa. [*As in: 'Ta-daaa' reveal*]

**SHAUN**: Ah, Pete. I should have known.

*He goes to pick up his shears.*

**SHEEP THREE**: [*to* **PETE**] Tell him to get on with it.

**PETE**: Alright, alright.

**SHEEP THREE**: I've got a hot date.

**PETE**: Keep your wool on.

**SHEEP THREE**: I've gotta look my best.

**PETE**: Don't get your tail in a twist. [*To* **SHAUN**] Baaaa. Baaaa.

**SHAUN**: Ooh, a hot date. Certainly. Come this way, madam.

**SHEEP THREE**: [*to* **PETE**] Better be good. [*To* **SHAUN**] Baaaa.

***SONG FIVE: 'Shaun's Night Shear'***

**SHAUN**: [*to* **SHEEP THREE**] *Kindly pop up there.*
[*To* **PETE**] *Special cut for you.*
[*To* **SHEEP THREE**] *Would you please incline your head?*

**SHEEP THREE**: *Manners are so rare!*
*Very welcome, too.*
*Lucky ewes are that well bred.*

**SHAUN**: *Clip, clip, snip, snip, snip…*

**PETE**: [*to* **SHEEP THREE**] *All the others will be fawning*
*When they see you in the morning!*

**SHAUN**: *Now I can show them all how I do it.*
*Part of our job should be Art – that's how I view it.*
*Clip, clip, snip, snip, snip, take a bow!*

*Sung simultaneously:*

**PETE & SHEEP THREE**: *Shearing in a chair!*
*What a special treat!*
*This should be in 'Ewe Idea'.*
*Soon your/our woolly hair*

**SHEEP THREE**: *Yeah!*

**PETE & SHEEP THREE**: *Will be nice and neat*

**SHEEP THREE**: *Sweet!*

**PETE & SHEEP THREE**: *Kiss curl is the look this year.*

**SHAUN**: *Now I can show them all how I do it.*
*Part of our job should be Art – that's how I view it.*

**PETE & SHEEP THREE**: *Snip.*
**SHAUN**: *Clip.*
**PETE & SHEEP THREE**: *Snip.*
**SHAUN**: *Clip.*
**PETE & SHEEP THREE**: *Clip.*
**SHAUN**: *Snip.*
**PETE & SHEEP THREE**: *Clip.*
**SHAUN**: *Snip.*
**PETE & SHEEP THREE**: *Clip.*
**SHAUN**: *Snip.*
**PETE & SHEEP THREE**: *Clip.*
**SHAUN**: *There!*
*I can find a style to suit ya.*
**PETE & SHEEP THREE**: *We have seen the shearing future!*

*Sung simultaneously:*

**SHAUN**: *Go, Shaun, go!*
*This is what I came for.*
*Go, Shaun…*
**PETE & SHEEP THREE**: *Baaa ba ba baaa ba baaa, etc.*

*The lights snap to full.*

**RATSO** *appears in his full night-time attire. Jammies, dressing-gown, nightcap and gumboots. During this scene,* **SHEEP THREE** *slowly backs out.*

**RATSO**: What in blazes is going on here? What's all this noise? It's the middle of the night! What are you doing back in this shed? And what are you doing to that sheep?
**SHAUN**: I can explain.
**RATSO**: I don't want your explanation. Trust me, I've seen enough. I've had enough.

**SHAUN**: But, Ratso...

**RATSO**: You've done yer dash, mate. I won't have this in me shed. I've got sheep that think they're dogs. I've got shearers that can't fill their quotas. The shed's come to a standstill. And it's all because of that blooming sheep-sheep of yours.

**PETE** *taps* **SHAUN** *on the shoulder.*

**SHAUN**: [*to* **PETE**] Not now, Pete. [*To* **RATSO**] I promise. What if I just work at night? I could fill my quota.

**RATSO**: Night, day. No way. You're upsetting the apple cart.

*Again* **PETE** *taps* **SHAUN** *on the shoulder.*

**SHAUN**: Later, Pete. [*To* **RATSO**] I'm not a bad apple, Ratso. There's nothing wrong with sheep looking smart. And I just have to shear.

**RATSO**: Shear? Shear?! What you do isn't shearing! What do you think this is? Harriette's Hair Salon? [*Or insert a local hairdresser reference.*]

**PETE** *taps* **SHAUN** *on the shoulder on the word 'salon'.*

**SHAUN**: Peter. Enough!

**RATSO**: You're a shearer, not a hairdresser.

**SHAUN**: Well, maybe you and your shearers should have a look at the way you're treating the sheep. Manhandling them.

**RATSO**: What? What are you implying? Listen, mate, you're trespassing on private property.

**SHAUN**: Have you ever asked the sheep how they're feeling? Have you? Come on, Ratso. Pete does.

**RATSO**: Listen, Mr Gifted and Talented, you haven't got a job here and I'm gonna make sure you don't get a job anywhere! You're barred!

**PETE**: Baaaa.

**RATSO**: Yes. Baaaaared. Get out. Get out! Get out!

**SHAUN** *and* **PETE** *leave the shed.*

**PETE** *taps* **SHAUN** *on the shoulder but* **SHAUN** *is too wrapped up in his own monologue.*

**SHAUN**: Well, Pete. Can't say we didn't try. Maybe we could get work somewhere else, in another shed. But when word gets out, no-one'll hire us. If we're too different for this shed, the others will probably be the same. They all follow each other like sheep. No offence.

**PETE**: Baaa.

**SHAUN**: Maybe I should just give up and try a totally different career. Open up a business or something. But what kind, Pete? A hardware shop? Nah. Boring.

**PETE** *taps* **SHAUN** *on the shoulder once more.*

**PETE**: Baa-baa. [*As in: Barber*]

**SHAUN***'s not listening.*

**SHAUN**: A coffee shop maybe? Nah. Don't like coffee.

**PETE**: Baa-baa.

**SHAUN**: A kebab shop?

**PETE** *gives* **SHAUN** *'the look'.*

**SHAUN**: Maybe not.

**PETE**: Baa-baa.

**SHAUN**: What?

**PETE**: Baa-baa.

**SHAUN**: Hey?

**PETE**: Barber!

*All of a sudden* **SHAUN** *realises what* **PETE** *has been trying to tell him all along.*

**SHAUN**: For sheep! Pete! You're an absolute genius!

**PETE**: Meh.

**SHAUN**: That's my specialty. They've never seen anything like it in this town. Come on, Pete, let's get this show on the road.

**PETE** *and* **SHAUN** *go to exit.*

## Scene Five

*On the farm. Later.*

**BRUTE** *enters, barking.* **TINY** *joins him, barking.*

**BRUTE & TINY**: Woof woof woof… Arrf arrrrf!

**SHAUN**: Righto, we're going.

**SHAUN** *exits.*

**BRUTE**: Woof. Get orf our property. You've been barred.

**TINY**: Arrf. We don't need your kind round here.

**PETE**: Yeah yeah. Keep your fur on, dogs.

**TINY**: You're not welcome.

**PETE**: We're outta here. Shaun and Pete have got plans. Who needs your shed? Not us. You just wait and see!

**BRUTE & TINY**: Woof woof. Arfff arfff.

**PETE** *points to some droppings on the ground.*

**PETE**: Look. Maltesers.

**PETE** *exits. The dogs rush to eat the Maltesers and are shocked to be eating sheep poo.*

**BRUTE**: Tiny, it's sheep poo!

**TINY**: I've had worse.

**FANG** *enters.*

**BRUTE**: Fang!

**TINY**: Hey, Fang, how was the vet?

**FANG**: Don't want to talk about it. Grrrr. What was that sheep doing in here?

**BRUTE**: Its owner calls it a sheep-sheep. They wanted to get a job shearing here, with us. Reckons it's as good as us sheepdogs.

**FANG**: No way.

**TINY**: It did a pretty good job though, that sheep-sheep.

**BRUTE**: Tiny. Get a grip. It's our job. Rounding up sheep.

**FANG**: It sure is, Brute. And don't you forget it, Tiny.

***SONG SIX: 'Sheepdogs' Life'***

**FANG**: *We're born and we're bred just to do one thing:*
*To show everybody that dogs are king.*
*Cos it's a sheepdog's life,*
*And our life is the best.*

**ALL**: *Ruff! We're the best!*

**FANG**: *And it was going just fine,*
*So why are the sheep unimpressed?*

**FANG**: [*howling*] *Oww!*

**BRUTE**: *Oww!*

**TINY**: *Oww!*

**FANG**: *Oww!*

**ALL**: *Oww!*

**FANG**: [*spoken*] Blind Tiny Footsteps.

*Harmonica break.*

**BRUTE**: [*sung*] *And as for that sheep-sheep, I hate to boast,*
*But he will end up as the Sunday roast!*
*Can't have our sheepdog's life,*
*He is not one of us.*

**ALL**: *Not one of us!*

**BRUTE**: *And the hairs on my neck tell me*
*This situation is sus.*
**FANG**: *Midnight (Sheepdog's life)*
*All alone at the station (Sheepdog's life)*
*Has the boss lost his marbles? (Sheepdog's life)*
*Is the world going bats?*
**ALL**: *Yep. World's gone bats.*
**BRUTE**: *There's only one thing I hate more than Pete –*
*And that's cats!*

## Scene Six

*On the farm. Morning.*

*Sunrise.*

*Morning sounds: a rooster, cockatoos, a cacophony of bird noises. Sheep noises.*

**SHEEP THREE** *is in the fenced-off paddock, awaiting round-up.*

**SHEEP FOUR** *enters and jumps into the paddock and parades her new do.*

**SHEEP THREE**: Shivering sheep dip! How did you get that look?
**SHEEP FOUR**: What look?
**SHEEP THREE**: That's a Shaun cut. And Shaun's been fired.
**SHEEP FOUR**: I didn't get it from here.
**SHEEP THREE**: Whheerreee did you get it?
**SHEEP FOUR**: Shaun's Sheep Salon.
**SHEEP THREE**: Salon?
**SHEEP FOUR**: Salon, yes. He's opened up in town. Shaun's Sheep Salon.
**SHEEP THREE**: OMG. I need another cut. Do they do perms?

**SHEEP FOUR**: They even do waxing.
**SHEEP THREE**: Oooh.
**SHEEP FOUR**: And they have an opening special. Cup of tea and a lambington.
**SHEEP THREE**: Ooh... where is it?
**SHEEP FOUR**: Between Clive the butcher and the saleyards.
**SHEEP THREE**: Where?
**SHEEP FOUR**: Opposite BBQ's Galore.
**SHEEP THREE**: Oh... I know where that is. The Red Meat District.
**SHEEP FOUR**: So spread the news. Best joint in town. Shaun's Sheep Salon.

> **SHEEP FOUR** *exits.* **SHEEP THREE** *jumps the fence and bleats loudly.*

**SHEEP THREE**: Girls! BFFs. Have I got some news for you...

> **TINY** *and* **FANG** *enter. They have overheard the sheep talking.*

**SHAUN**: Hey, Tiny. Did you hear that?
**TINY**: Yeah. Those sheep are getting haircuts from Shaun and he's got his own salon.
**FANG**: Boss isn't gonna be happy.
**TINY**: Why don't we go, Fang?
**FANG**: Where?
**TINY**: To Shaun's Sheep Salon.
**FANG**: Why?
**TINY**: To get a haircut.
**FANG**: Are you mad? We're dogs.
**TINY**: I work hard, Fang. I think I deserve a bit of a treatment.
**FANG**: Oh, Tiny. We can't do that. Our bosses'll go bananas.
**TINY**: Come on, Fang. We're not doing nothin' wrong. Just getting a little pampering done. Besides, after all you went through at the vet. Don't you think you deserve a special treat?

**FANG**: Oh, I don't know, Tiny.
**TINY**: Come on. We can leave them a note.
**FANG**: Ooh.
**TINY**: Come on, Fang.
**FANG**: Ahhh.
**TINY**: Just this once.
**FANG**: Ahhh.
**TINY**: A little trim?
**FANG**: Ohhh, alright! Hang on. Who's gonna write the note?

*They exit for the salon.*

## Scene Seven

*On the farm. Same day a little bit later.*

*No sounds of sheep at all.*

**BUNGO** *enters.*

**BUNGO**: Strewth! Boss!

**RATSO** *enters.*

**RATSO**: What?
**BUNGO**: Problem.
**RATSO**: Problem?
**BUNGO**: No sheep.
**RATSO**: What do you mean no sheep?
**BUNGO**: No sheep!
**RATSO**: No sheep? If there's no sheep there's no shearing. And if there's no shearing…
**BUNGO & RATSO**: Strewth!
**RATSO**: This place has gone to rack and ruin. Better get the dogs to look for them. Brute!

**BUNGO**: Fang!

**RATSO**: Brute!

**BUNGO**: Fang!

**RATSO**: Hang on a minute. Where are the bloomin' dogs?

**BRUTE** *enters.*

**RATSO**: Brute! Where have you been?

**BRUTE** *drops a note at their feet.* **RATSO** *reads it out.*

**RATSO**: 'Gone to get a trim. Love, Tiny and Fang.' A trim?

**BUNGO**: Fang? Strewth!

**RATSO**: This day's getting worse and worse. Come on, Brute. Let's round 'em up, let's bring 'em home.

*Andrew James (left) as Ratso and Todd Keys as Brute in the 2015 Monkey Baa Theatre Company production at the Lend Lease Darling Quarter Theatre, Sydney.* (Photo: Heidrun Löhr)

**BRUTE** *runs off.*

**RATSO**: Not so fast, ya mangy mutt.

*They all race off after him.*

## Scene Eight

*Afternoon. Shaun's Sheep Salon, interior.*

*A bright, happy day.*

*The sounds of hairdryers, the 'tsss' of a curling tong, razors being sharpened. The spinning of a chair.*

**PETE** *and* **SHAUN** *reveal the salon. Lots of sheep sounds coming from the street.*

***SONG SEVEN: 'New Salon Song'***

*Instrumental intro for setting up the salon scenery.*

**PETE**: *We showed the shearers that we left behind:*
*We do things our way cos we're more refined.*
*Business is booming and I think we'll find*
*That the plan is A-okay.*

**SHAUN**: *The sheep look bonza and their wool is top!*
*I'm shearing nine to five and I can't stop!*
*This town no longer has an empty shop –*
*Shaun and Pete have shown the way.*

**PETE & SHAUN**: *Cos we're the Dream Team.*

**SHAUN**: *Open the doors!*

**PETE & SHAUN**: *We're called the Dream Team.*

**PETE**: *Simply because.*

**PETE & SHAUN**: *The sheep all flock here: a never-ending stream,*
*Just to meet the Dream Team.*

**SHAUN**: *And each new customer receives a treat:*
*Those yummy lambingtons they love to eat!*
*Three thousand sheep are waiting in the street,*
*Just for me to do my stuff!*

**PETE**: *What good's a stylist in an old tin shed?*
*Don't be afraid to come to us instead.*
*We welcome every woolly quadruped.*

**SHEEP FOUR**: *And we cannot get enough.*

**ALL**: *Cos we're/they're the Dream Team,*
*Give us/'em a try.*
*Check out the Dream Team,*
*Cut and blow dry.*
*You're gonna feel like the cat that got the cream,*
*When you meet the Dream Team.*

**BRUTE** *enters the salon.*

**SHAUN**: I'm terribly sorry. We can't do any more dogs.

**PETE**: Baaaa.

**SHAUN**: It's a sheep salon, Pete.

**BRUTE**: Woof. Grrrr.

**SHAUN**: I guess we could fit you in.

**BRUTE**: Grrrr.

**SHAUN**: You do look a little tense. How about a shampoo and a flea treatment? Here, boy, fetch. And we'll do the worms as well.

*Before* **BRUTE** *can protest,* **PETE** *has put him in the barber chair.*

**SHAUN**: [*to* **BRUTE**] There's no reason why you can't look gorgeous too.

**PETE**: Baaaa.

**SHAUN**: *And yes, the Dream Team*
*Even do dogs.*
*We are the Dream Team,*
*Check out our blogs!*

**BRUTE**: *And when my hair's done, I will look supreme.*

**SHAUN**: *Gotta love the Dream,*

**PETE**: *Gotta love the Team,*

**ALL**: *Gotta love the Dream Team!*

*As the music continues, it is interrupted by* **RATSO***'s entrance.*

**RATSO**: Brute? What in blazes is going on here? Doggone it!

**SHAUN**: Ratso. Welcome.

**RATSO**: Forget your welcome. Where's me dog gone? Brute! Brute?

*The barber chair spins with* **BRUTE** *in it, having his hair done.*

**BRUTE**: Woof!

**RATSO**: Et tu, Brute?

**BRUTE**: Woof!

**RATSO**: Ah, Brute, even my dog has gone to the dogs. I must be dreaming. And where have all the sheep gone?

*The chair spins again and reveals a* **SHEEP** *with a great do.*

**SHEEP**: [**BOB**] Baaa.

**RATSO**: This is getting ridiculous. No dogs, no sheep. Well… if I've got nothing else, I've got me mates. At least ya mates don't cut and run.

*The chair spins once more and* **BIG BOB** *is in it, with a cape.*

**BIG BOB**: Bonjour, Ratso.

**RATSO**: Oh, Bob. Comrade. Mate.

**BIG BOB**: Sorry, Ratso. B&S ball's coming up.

**RATSO**: What are you doing to me, mate?

**BIG BOB**: I needed a bit of spit and polish.

**RATSO**: Give me strength. When will this day ever end?

**SHAUN**: You must admit, he does look sensational.

**PETE**: Baaa.

**SHAUN**: What do you think, Ratso?

**RATSO**: What do I think? What do I think? You know what I think? I'll tell ya what I think! The world's gone loco! That's what I think!

**RATSO** *storms out.*

**BIG BOB, SHAUN** *and* **PETE** *are left in the salon, not sure quite what to do. A bit embarrassed.*

**SHAUN**: We can't let him go.

**BIG BOB**: He's the best shearer in town.

**SHAUN**: And we've got sheep coming out of our ears. We need help.

**BIG BOB**: Well, you'd better get him back in here.

**SHAUN**: How?

**PETE**: Baaa. Baaaa. Baaaa.

**SHAUN**: Yeah. We could give that a go.

**BIG BOB**: Give what a go?

**SHAUN** *and* **PETE** *hang at the door to watch as* **BIG BOB** *morphs into* **BRUTE**.

## Scene Nine

*The lights come up on…*

*Shaun's Sheep Salon, exterior.*

**RATSO** *is sitting on an apple crate.*

**BRUTE** *exits the salon with tongs and drops them at* **RATSO**'*s feet.*

**RATSO** *throws them away.*

**RATSO**: Get away with ya, Brute.

**BRUTE** *brings them back and sits near* **RATSO***.*

**RATSO**: Brute. Knock it off.

**RATSO** *throws the tongs away again.* **BRUTE** *returns them and sits.*

**RATSO**: Brute!

**RATSO** *throws the tongs for a third time.* **BRUTE** *stays put.* **SHAUN** *comes out of the salon.*

**SHAUN**: Ratso? Ratso, why don't you come and join the salon?

**RATSO**: You want me to... Nah... the shearing shed's the place for me.

**SHAUN**: It's not about the shed. You'll always be the best shearer.

**RATSO**: Fat lot of good that's gonna do me. There's no sheep left to shear.

**SHAUN**: There's plenty to shear. They're all sitting waiting for a new 'do'.

**RATSO**: I don't know anything about 'new do's'.

**SHAUN**: Doesn't have to be anything fancy. They just wanna look different, they wanna be themselves.

**RATSO**: I'm too set in me ways.

**SHAUN**: I can't do it all by myself, Ratso.

**RATSO**: I told ya. I can't do those fancy-shmancy cuts.

**SHAUN**: They don't all want fancy-shmancy cuts. Some of them just want short back and sides.

**RATSO**: Really?

**SHAUN**: Come on, Ratso. We want you.

**RATSO**: But I'm too old to change.

**SHAUN**: I need the best and that's you.

**PETE** *is watching this exchange. He goes and picks up some shears and drops them in front of* **RATSO**.

**PETE**: Baaaa.

*All of a sudden* **RATSO** *hears and understands* **PETE**. *He picks up the shears.*

**RATSO**: A new team?

**PETE**: Baaaa.

**SHAUN**: How about it, Ratso?

**PETE**: Baaaa.

**BRUTE**: Woof.

**RATSO**: Alright, I'll give it a burl.

**PETE**, **SHAUN** *and* **BRUTE** *let out baas, woofs and hoorays.*

**RATSO**: But I'm not doing no perms.

**RATSO** *finally joins them in the salon.*

*Shaun's Sheep Salon, interior.*

***REPRISE: 'Dream Team'***

**ALL**: *He's joined the Dream Team,*
*All thanks to Pete.*
**RATSO**: *The Flaming Dream Team,*
**SHAUN**: *Now it's complete.*
**ALL**: *The greatest thing since*
*The Snowy Mountain Scheme.*
*The Shaggy Gully Dream Team.*

***SONG: Finale***

SHAUN, PETE, RATSO *and* BIG BOB.

*Music is the same as the opening sequence.*

**ALL**: *So thank you, everybody,*
*Our story's near the end.*
*We learnt a new way to shear a sheep*
*And how to stick by a friend.*

**SHAUN**: *Old Ratso's in the salon too,*

**PETE**: *And, as he told reporters:*

**RATSO**: *In just one year of Shaun's new plan*

**BRUTE**: *The yield fell by three quarters.*

**ALL**: *The animals in the zoo*
*Now come for haircuts too!*
*So it's: Hoo-roo! Hoo-roo!*
*Hoo-roo! Hoo-roo!*
*Lions, tigers, monkeys in a tree,*
*Keep 'em coming till we break for a nice hot cup of billy tea!*

**RATSO**: *And a slice of quiche for me!*

*Blackout.*

*In the dark we hear animal sounds: elephants, birds, sheep, cows.*

THE END